Gauguin

ELEANOR MARRACK

BISON GROUP

First published in 1993 by
Bison Books Ltd
Kimbolton House
117A Fulham Road
London SW3 6RL

ISBN 0-86124-722-1

Printed in Hong Kong

LIST OF PLATES

PAUL GAUGUIN

1848-1903

Paul Gauguin was in no doubt of his own significance in the artistic history of his times. He consciously cultivated a high public profile during his life as a working artist, both through the amount of written exegesis he devoted to his work – he seemed quite unconvinced that the public would be capable of grasping what he was about without guidance – and through the dramatic events of his life, above all the much-publicized flight from European civilization to take up an idealized, primitive existence in Tahiti. He fostered the idea of two opposing natures, the sensitive and the savage, in eternal conflict within himself and liked to quote Degas' description of him as the 'loup maigre' of La Fontaine's fable; the wolf who prefers to starve rather than submit to a collar and chain.

This predilection for image-building, and Gauguin's conscious use of publicity, his courting of critics and other literary figures to serve as intermediaries between his art and his public, makes any detached assessment of his place in the history of art a particularly difficult exercise. While contemporaries such as Monet, Pissarro, Cézanne, and Signac regarded Gauguin with suspicion, others hailed his work as revolutionary. The critic Albert Aurier, one of the leaders of the Symbolist movement in literature, placed Gauguin at the start of a Symbolist movement in painting and stressed the innovatory qualities of his work, which he regarded as marking a decisive break with the naturalism and objec-

tivity that was the aim of the Impressionists. Recent commentators have tended to regard as Gauguin's most important legacy his use of color for its decorative and emotional effect, his liberation of form and color from the Impressionists' preoccupation with the rendering of naturalistic effects – a process already begun by that other great Post-Impressionist painter, Cézanne.

Born in Paris in 1848, Eugène Henri Paul Gauguin moved with his family a year later to Peru, his mother's country of birth, when his father, a Republican journalist, fled into political exile. Clovis Gauguin died on the ship taking them to South America, and the young Paul spent the next four years there with his mother and older sister, a formative experience that seems to have left him with a restless taste for the exotic. On the family's return to France Paul was sent to school in Orléans and then attended a pre-naval college in Paris. His mother worked as a dressmaker to support the family and at some point met the financier Gustave Arosa, whom she left as guardian to her two children on her death in 1867, by which time Gauguin was at sea as a merchant seaman.

Returning to Paris in 1872, Gauguin began work as a stockbroker with the support of the influential Arosa. He seems to have been successful in his chosen line of business, and rose rapidly in the series of finance firms for which he worked between 1872 and 1883. At about the same time as he began work he also started to paint in his spare time with one of his colleagues, Emile Schuffenecker, with whom he attended evening life classes at the large and informal Académie Colarossi. Gauguin's earliest works are in the landscape tradition of the Barbizon school, but his early taste was also no doubt influenced by his guardian Arosa, whose collection of contemporary paintings included works by Courbet, Corot, Delacroix and Pissarro, and who seems to have been genuinely interested in work that fell well outside the range of the Salon, the official, state-sponsored, annual art exhibition. At some point in the early 1870s Arosa introduced Gauguin to Pissarro, who was one of the prime movers behind what came to be called the first Impressionist exhibition in 1874. This was mounted by a group of young artists which also included Monet, Renoir, Sisley, Cézanne, Morisot, and Degas, with the aim of finding an alternative outlet for their work to the conservative Salon. The major changes they introduced to the landscape genre, including a lighter palette, freer paint handling, and the use of informal, usually *plein-air* settings, resonates through the work of the young Gauguin. At the very end of his life he again expressed his indebtedness to Pissarro, whom he described as his 'master' and whose importance, he felt, had been underestimated. It was from Pissarro that he learned to abandon blacks, browns, and ochers and to concentrate on the three primary colors and their main derivatives. In the late 1870s he began to depict angular views, to use broken color and to adopt the same kind of everyday subject matter as the Impressionists.

Another and more immediately influential introduction in 1872, however, was to the young Danish woman Mette Sofie Gad, whom Gauguin married the following year. For ten years the couple lived an apparently unexceptional, prosperous, bourgeois life in Paris, with Gauguin devoting his Sundays to *plein-air* painting and Mette giving birth to their five children, two of whom were named Aline and Clovis after Gauguin's parents. By 1879 Gauguin's finances were sufficiently comfortable for him to begin making his own collection of Impressionist works, and he was also invited to submit work to the Impressionist exhibition of that and the following year.

In 1881 Pissarro's dealer, Paul Durand-Ruel, bought three paintings for a handsome 1500 francs, and Gauguin received his first unequivocal critical acclaim for his robust *Study of a Nude* (1880) from the critic J-K Huysmans, who greeted it as 'a bold and truthful canvas.' His landscapes of this time reflect an increasing awareness among many of the Impressionist group of the limitations of outdoor painting, and the impossibility of making a direct and immediate record of what they saw while the particular fleeting effect of light lasted. Both Gauguin and Pissarro took a keen interest in the technical progress being made by Cézanne at this time, and the three may have worked together at Pissarro's home at Pontoise. Cézanne was in the process of developing his very individual system of regular parallel brushstrokes to give density and unity to a painting's surface while retaining the spontaneity of the initial inspiration, and Gauguin wrote jokingly to Pissarro: 'If [Cézanne] should find the recipe for concentrating the full expression of all his sensations into a single and unique procedure, try, I beg you, to get him to talk about it in his sleep . . .' Failing to persuade the notoriously recalcitrant older artist to discuss his methods, Gauguin fell back on studying Cézanne's work and by the mid-1880s owned six canvases. In this he was ahead of most of his contemporaries, and it is a mark of Gauguin's own originality that he understood and appreciated what Cézanne, always the most contentious of the Impressionists, was in the process of achieving. Cézanne's powerful vision and forceful use of color already held more appeal for Gauguin than the atmospheric delicacy of Monet or Pissarro.

A financial crisis on the Paris stock market in 1882, coinciding with the crash of the Union Fédérale bank, substantially reduced Gauguin's earnings, and it was perhaps in the light of this that he decided to abandon his stockbroking activities and commit himself wholeheartedly to an artistic career. He was confident that, with the right administrative skills and the right contacts, he would be able to conquer the art market and make painting a viable full-time enterprise. Mette was considerably less enthusiastic and, after a year of cheap living in Rouen, removed herself and three of the children to her parents' home in Copenhagen, where Gauguin followed her a month later. While his wife, from her limited experience of him, might with some justice view Gauguin as the model family man who had suddenly and unexpectedly abandoned the comforts of bourgeois life for an altogether chancier existence, an overview of his life as a whole shows a different pattern. From that perspective, the ten-year period of settled and monied domesticity represents a calm hiatus in an otherwise turbulent and uncertain career. Gauguin seems to have subscribed vigorously to the notion prevalent at the time that artistic genius could not thrive within the confines of normal social ties and responsibilities.

The period in Copenhagen was an isolated and unhappy one. The climate was little suited to outdoor painting; Mette's family disapproved of his choice of occupation; and he felt cut off from the cultural center of Paris, describing himself for the first, but by no means last, time as a 'martyr' of painting. Nonetheless his output rose dramatically; in 1885 he painted about 50 pictures, compared with only about a dozen in the years when he was exhibiting with the Impressionists. These, such as *Cows in a Landscape* (1888), were mainly in the impressionist landscape tradition with which he had already aligned himself, but his letters reveal an increasing dissatisfaction with the rigorous naturalism that this entailed. To Schuffenecker he wrote: 'Don't perspire over a picture, a strong emotion can be translated immediately: dream on it and seek its simplest form.'

In this Gauguin seems to anticipate some of the concerns of Symbolism, initially a purely literary movement which grew out of a dissatisfaction with the naturalism of authors such as Zola who had dominated much nineteenth-century writing. In 1886 Jean Moréas published the *Symbolist Manifesto*, which first expressly articulated and gave a name to concerns which had animated the literary world for some years. Literary Symbolism sought to explore and express the changing, subtle states of the human psyche through symbol and metaphor, abolishing the separation between subject and object and subscribing to a metaphysical conception of the universe. In the same year the young critic Félix Fénéon, while acclaiming Seurat's pointillist work *A Sunday Afternoon at the Grande Jatte* as a landmark in avant-garde painting which outstripped the 'fleeting glimpses' of Impressionism, also praised Gauguin for his unusual density of color.

Gauguin returned to France in 1885 and showed a total of 19 pictures in the eighth and final Impressionist exhibition of the following year. By then the stranglehold of the Salon had been reduced and the impetus which had fueled the first group show had largely dissipated, the inclusion of new members such as Seurat and Signac indicating a change of emphasis. Gauguin spent the summer of 1886 in the Breton port of Pont-Aven, a seasonal gathering-place for artists, in the hope of living more cheaply. He subscribed to the prevailing preoccupation (already largely anachronistic) in the literary and artistic world with a 'primitive' way of life to be found there, and the paintings he produced at this time are highly selective, focusing on traditional religious festivals and folk costumes. *Four Breton Women* (1886) shows Gauguin moving away from established impressionist practice and aiming at a more synthetic effect, but using forms and colors rather than the unifying brush stroke of Cézanne. Similar Breton themes inspired the pottery that was the main product of the next few months. Gauguin's finances, as so often from now on, were in a critical state, and it seems that he had high hopes of making ceramics a profitable enterprise. He turned out 55 pieces in the course of a month, but his expectation of a lively market proved ill-founded. Continuing money problems and a short-lived panic about a possible war with Germany motivated a trip to the Caribbean island of Martinique, a French protectorate, in 1887. The genuinely primitive way of life and dazzling colors Gauguin found there inspired a further stage in his emancipation from Pissarro's influence. *Martinique Landscape* (1887), with its saturated color and restricted palette, seems more concerned with surface patterns than with the rendering of atmosphere or landscape.

A second summer in Brittany in 1888 confirmed this development. By this time Gauguin had met both Emile Bernard and Vincent van Gogh, painters interested in the literary avant-garde and the application of general laws to art. In a letter to Schuffenecker, Gauguin wrote of Brittany: 'When my clogs echo on this granite earth, I hear the dull, muffled, powerful note that I seek in painting.' The thorough-going abandonment of naturalism in *Vision after the Sermon* (1888), while conventionally hailed as a turning point, in fact reflects a synthesis of elements already noticeable in Gauguin's work. The flattening of space, the flat blocks of non-naturalistic color and the evocative use of traditional peasant costume have been seen before; what is new is the overtly symbolic nature of the subject matter. Gauguin conveys the effect of a religious experience on a group of peasant women by expressing it as a vision of biblical wrestlers evoked in their minds by the sermon they have just heard. The very idea of painting a vision ran counter to the aims of Impressionism, and Pissarro recognized at once that this painting represented a professional and temperamental parting of the ways for himself and his pupil. Gauguin was creating a pictorial language based on idea and symbol rather than perception and sensation, and it was this that inspired the young poet and art critic Albert Aurier to hail him as the 'uncontested initiator of Symbolist painting.'

At the end of 1888 Gauguin accepted an invitation from van Gogh, who had long cherished the idea of a community of artists, to live and work with him in Arles. Gauguin's motives were probably more mercenary, as Vincent's brother Theo promised him a monthly income in exchange for a picture. The period in Arles, like the preceding one in Brittany, was an intensely productive time, although Gauguin did not find the same inspiration in the Provençal landscape as van Gogh and turned instead to the local women for much of his subject matter. The fundamentally differing philosophies and the antipathetic temperaments of the two artists caused a series of confrontations, however, and the visit ended dramatically with van Gogh confined to hospital, having severed his own ear, and Gauguin back in Paris.

The Exposition Universelle of 1889, a celebration of the centenary of the French Revolution which included an exhibition of colonial life, reawakened Gauguin's latent enthusiasm for what he perceived to be the primitive and colorful lifestyle to be found in the tropics. In a letter to Bernard in summer 1890 he referred to his wish to 'set up a studio in the tropics . . . I can buy a hut of the kind you saw at the Exposition Universelle.' A roughly contemporary letter to van Gogh finds Gauguin projecting an image of the artist as outsider that was increasingly to dominate his life and work in his later years. 'Alas, I see myself condemned to be less and less understood, and I must resign myself to following my path alone, dragging out an existence without family, like a pariah . . . the savage will return to the wilderness'; this despite his growing reputation as a leading avant-garde painter and his wife's continuing, if distant, loyalty.

Tahiti was the final choice of destination, partly influenced by Pierre Loti's popular novel *The Marriage of Loti*, published in 1880, which told of a sailor's marriage to a 14-year-old Tahitian and evoked a society peopled with beautiful and available women. In order to raise funds for his trip, Gauguin began consciously to court the avant-garde writers and critics who had already started to acclaim his work. Many of the paintings produced at this time seem to have been aimed specifically at this small, well-informed audience. *The Loss of Virginity* (1890) is a reworking of the theme of Manet's *Olympia* with symbolic overtones: Manet's black cat becomes a fox, described by Gauguin as a 'symbol of perversity'; the red-tipped cyclamen alludes to the girl's defloration; and the alternative title *The Awakening of Spring* evokes an increasingly common theme in Gauguin's work from now on, the idea of personal liberation through sex.

Much of Gauguin's posthumous reputation rests on the works he produced in Tahiti where, apart from a two-year return to Paris in 1893-95, he stayed until 1902, finally moving to Hivaoa where he died a year later. The cult that he generated, of the artist as loner working outside the constraints of western civilization and the conventions of realism in order to ensure the purity of his art, gained wide currency in the twentieth century, when Gauguin was hailed as the forerunner of Expressionist art. In fact, however, the self-imposed isolation, after nearly 20 years as a working artist and with a number of important patrons and supporters to his credit, was at best a sporadic affair. He remained in correspondence with friends, acquaintances, and dealers in Paris, sent his paintings and wood carvings back, often with elaborate instructions for their promotion and sale, and wrote a number of texts intended to complement and explain his work. Tahiti was far more westernized than Gauguin had expected, and as in Brittany he resorted to the depiction of a mythical primitivism, based on half-forgotten tradition and fictionalized accounts like *The Marriage of Loti*, and also on a collection of photographs, drawings, and prints which he had brought with him from France and which reveal him to have been far more dependent on western sources than he liked to maintain.

It took some time before Gauguin settled down and produced any largescale works, and the first of these made clear use of his collection of source material in a complex fusion of observation and artifice. Much of the early Tahitian work was unashamedly directed at a male consumer market. Throughout his career it was images of women on which Gauguin concentrated, and a painting such as *Vahine no te Vi* (1892) seems calculated to appeal to European bourgeois taste, with its straightforward image of a young girl, the first of a succession of native mistresses with whom Gauguin lived. When he sent this and seven other works to Copenhagen for exhibition in 1892, he provided his long-suffering wife with a gloss on their meaning and on the Tahitian titles that he had taken to giving them.

8

The two-year visit to Paris was marked by a critically acclaimed but financially unproductive one-man show and the final break with his wife and children. On Gauguin's final return to Tahiti, he found himself plagued by ill-health, the as-yet undiagnosed effects of syphilis, which finally caused his death in 1903. In his last years his mobility became severely restricted and his work was confined to a studio-based practice. This re-inforced the tendency he had already established in Paris to recycle ideas based on his own reconstruction of Tahitian tradition. Western influences also reappear: *Nave Nave Mahana* (1896), with its rough canvas and chalky paint resembling fresco, recalls the wall paintings of the nineteenth-century artist Puvis de Cha-vannes, while *Three Tahitians* (1899) reworks the traditional subject of the Three Graces.

Much of the late work is noticeably less focused and vital than that of the 1880s, but the move to Hivaoa produced a temporary renewal of Gauguin's creative energies, and in a painting such as *Contes Barbares* (1902) he equalled the ambition and stylistic force of earlier work. The two tranquil women, derived from Gauguin's photographs of the Javanese temple of Boro-budur, are brooded over by the crouching dwarflike figure in the background, who resembles a fox, the symbol of perversity, but who also bears the features of Gauguin's old painting companion Meyer de Haan. The contrast between the European perceived as a corrupting force and the innocence of the native women; the dual nature of woman as both pure and knowing; the allusive title as complex as the content of the painting; all are recurring themes in Gauguin's South Seas work, here presented as forcefully as ever.

In a letter of 1902 Gauguin wrote: 'You have known for a long time what it has been my aim to vindicate: the right to dare anything. My capacities (and the pecuniary difficulties in my life have interfered greatly with the carrying out of my task) have not allowed me to achieve a great result, but the mechanism has been set in motion nevertheless . . . The public owe me nothing since my pictorial *oeuvre* is only relatively good, but the painters of today who are benefiting from this new-born freedom do owe me something.' This is a surprisingly accurate self-assessment from a painter more normally noted for his self-aggrandizement. Gauguin's inventive originality did indeed have a decisive influence on much early twentieth-century art. His reputation was established when 227 of his paintings were shown at the Salon d'Automne in 1906. His work was a source of inspiration for both the Nabis and the Fauves and has been one of the major influences on the general non-naturalistic trend of twentieth-century art.

Self-Portrait with Halo, 1889
Oil on wood, 31¾×20¼ in (79.2×51.3 cm)
National Gallery of Art, Washington

GARDEN IN THE RUE CARCEL, 1881-2
Oil on canvas, 34¼×44⅞ in (87×114 cm)
Ny Carlsberg Glyptotek, Copenhagen

Right
STUDY OF A NUDE OR SUZANNE SEWING, 1880
Oil on canvas, 45¼×31½ in (115×80 cm)
Ny Carlsberg Glyptotek, Copenhagen

STILL LIFE WITH ORANGES, *c*.1881
Oil on canvas, 13×18¼ in
(33×46 cm)
Musée des Beaux-Arts, Rennes

COWS IN A LANDSCAPE, 1885
Oil on canvas, 25¼×31½ in (64×80 cm)
Museum Boymans van Beuningen, Rotterdam

FOUR BRETON WOMEN, 1886
Oil on canvas, 28⅜×35⅜ in (72×90 cm)
*Bayerischen Staatsgemäldesammlungen,
Munich*

MARTINIQUE LANDSCAPE, 1887
Oil on canvas, 45¾×35 in (115.5×89 cm)
National Gallery of Scotland, Edinburgh

BOYS WRESTLING, 1888
Oil on canvas, 36⅝×28¾ in (93×73 cm)
Josefowitz Collection

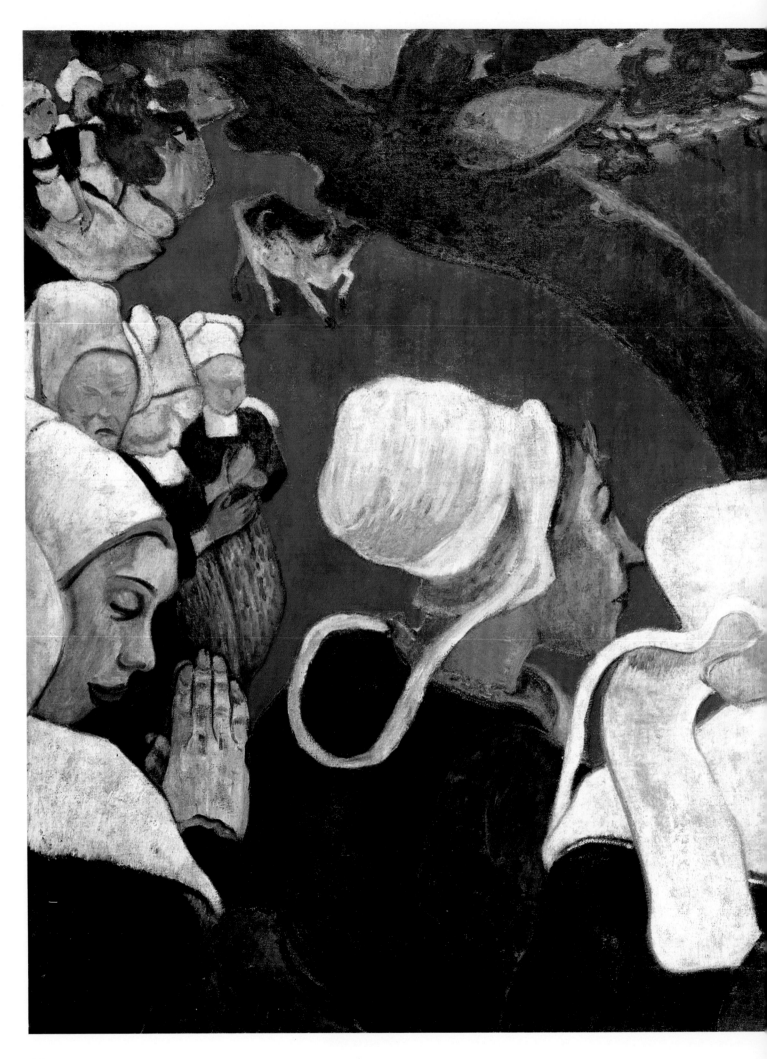

Vision After the Sermon or Jacob Wrestling
with the Angel, 1888
Oil on canvas, 28¾×36¼ in (73×92 cm)
National Gallery of Scotland

Madeleine Bernard, 1888
Oil on canvas, 28×22½ in (72×58 cm)
Musée de Grenoble

THE ALYSCAMPS, 1888
Oil on canvas, 36¼×28¾ in (92×73 cm)
Musée d'Orsay, Paris

26

YELLOW HAYSTACKS, 1889
Oil on canvas, 29×36⅝ in (73.5×93 cm)
Musée d'Orsay, Paris

Left
GREEN CHRIST (BRETON CALVARY), 1889
Oil on canvas, 36¼×28¾ in (92×73 cm)
Musées Royaux des Beaux-Arts de Belgique, Brussels

THE LOSS OF VIRGINITY or THE AWAKENING OF SPRING, 1890
Oil on canvas, 35½×51¼ in (90×130 cm)
Chrysler Museum, Norfolk, Virginia

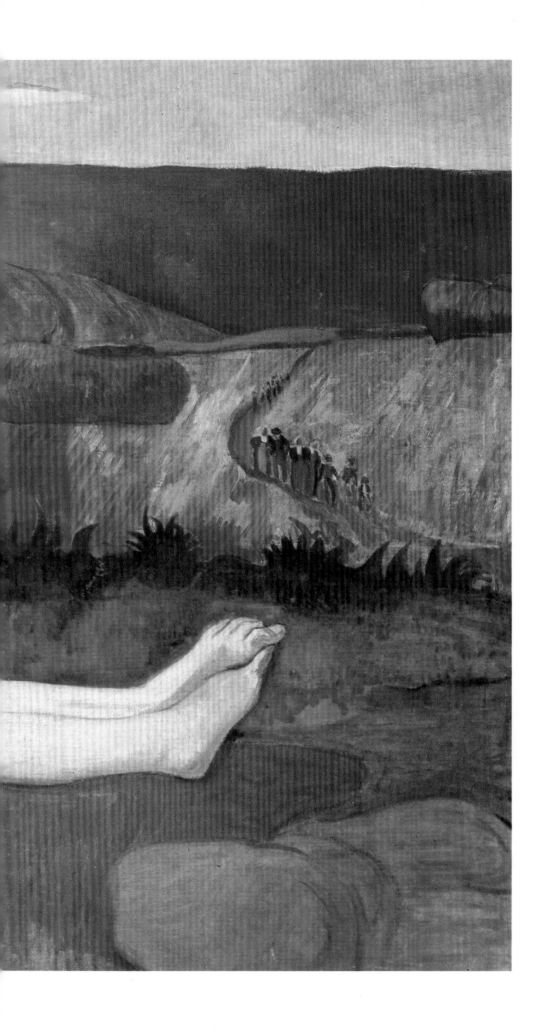

TAHITIAN LANDSCAPE, 1891
Oil on canvas, 26¾×36⅜ in
(68×92 cm)
Minneapolis Institute of Arts

Te Tiare Farani (The Flowers of France), 1891
Oil on canvas, 28⅜×36¼ in (72×92 cm)
Hermitage Museum, Leningrad

Right
Vahine no te Vi (Woman with a Mango), 1892
Oil on canvas, 28⅝×17½ in (72.7×44.5 cm)
Baltimore Museum of Art

Left
Nafea Faa Ipoipo (When will you marry?), 1892
Oil on canvas, 40×30½ in (101.5×77.5 cm)
Rudolph Staechelin Foundation, Basle

Below
Pape Moe (Mysterious Water), 1893
Oil on canvas, 39×29½ in (99×75 cm)
Private collection, Switzerland

MAHANA NO ATUA (DAY OF THE GOD), 1894
Oil on canvas, 26⅞×36 in (68.3×91.5 cm)
Art Institute of Chicago

UPAUPA SCHNEKLUD, 1894
Oil on canvas, 36½×28⅞ in (92.5×73.5 cm)
Baltimore Museum of Art

NAVE NAVE MAHANA
(WONDERFUL DAYS), 1896
Oil on canvas, 37×51¼ in
(94×130 cm)
Musée des Beaux-Arts, Lyons

Above
THREE TAHITIANS, 1899
Oil on canvas, 28¾×36 in (73×91 cm)
National Gallery of Scotland

Right
CONTES BARBARES (PRIMITIVE TALES), 1902
Oil on canvas, 51¾×35⅝ in (131.5×90.5 cm)
Folkwang Museum, Essen

ACKNOWLEDGMENTS

The publisher wishes to thank Martin Bristow, who designed this book, and the following agencies and institutions, who supplied illustrative material.

The Art Institute of Chicago: page 38

The Baltimore Museum of Art: pages 35, 39

Bayerischen Staatsgemäldesammlungen, Munich/ photo Artothek: pages 16-17

The Chrysler Museum, Norfolk, Virginia: pages 30-31

The Cleveland Museum of Art: page 27 (Gift of Mr and Mrs William Powell Jones, 78.63)

Folkwang Museum, Essen: page 43

Hermitage Museum, Leningrad/photo Scala: page 34

Josefowitz Collection: page 19

The Minneapolis Institute of Arts: page 32

Musée des Beaux-Arts de Lyon: pages 40-41

Musée des Beaux-Arts, Rennes/Bridgeman Art Library: pages 12-13

Museum Boymans-van Beuningen, Rotterdam: pages 14-15

Musée de Grenoble: page 24

Musée d'Orsay/photo RMN: pages 25, 29

Musées Royaux des Beaux-Arts de Belgique, Brussels: page 28

Narodni Gallery, Prague: page 26

National Gallery of Art, Washington: page 8 (Chester Dale Collection)

National Gallery of Scotland: pages 18, 22-23, 42

Ny Carlsberg Glyptotek, Copenhagen: pages 10, 11

Private Collection, Switzerland, page 37

Rudolf Staechelin Family Foundation, Basle/photo Hans Hinz: page 36

Vincent Van Gogh Foundation/National Museum Vincent Van Gogh, Amsterdam: pages 20-21